Infrastructure 2014

Shaping the Competitive City

Urban Land Institute

EY
Building a better
working world

CONTRIBUTING AUTHORS

Colin Galloway

Rachel MacCleery

ULI PRINCIPAL RESEARCHERS AND ADVISERS

Sara Hammerschmidt
Associate, Content

Basil Hallberg
Senior Associate, Content

Gesine Kippenberg
Cities Programme Manager

Rachel MacCleery
Senior Vice President, Content

EY ADVISERS

Howard Roth
Global Real Estate Leader

Malcolm Bairstow
Global and EMEA Infrastructure and Construction Leader

Bill Banks
Global Infrastructure Leader, Transactions Advisory and
    Government, and Asia-Pacific Leader

Rick Sinkuler
Global Real Estate Markets Leader
Global Real Estate Center

Michael Parker
Senior Managing Director and U.S. Infrastructure Advisory
    Leader
EY Infrastructure Advisors, LLC

Jay Gillespie
Vice President
EY Infrastructure Advisors, LLC

Rebecca Hiscock-Croft
Senior Strategic Analyst
EY Knowledge

Jill Maguire
Global Marketing Leader
Global Real Estate Center

BELDEN RUSSONELO STRATEGISTS ADVISERS

Nancy Belden
Partner

Emma Freeman
Associate Analyst

PRODUCTION STAFF

James A. Mulligan
Senior Editor

David James Rose
Managing Editor/Manuscript Editor

Betsy VanBuskirk
Creative Director

John Hall Design Group
Graphic Designer

Craig Chapman
Senior Director, Publishing Operations

Cover: Vancouver, British Columbia, Canada, has invested
in infrastructure to support high-density living.

Recommended bibliographical listing:
Urban Land Institute and EY. *Infrastructure 2014: Shaping the Competitive City*. Washington, D.C.: Urban Land Institute, 2014.

ISBN: 978-0-87420-351-6

Cover Letter

AROUND THE WORLD, communities are investing in infrastructure. Hundreds of billions are spent each year by countries around the globe maintaining existing infrastructure and expanding and enhancing systems. Despite the activity, there is always more to do, and nearly everywhere there is a sense that resources lag far behind the need.

But what does it all add up to? What role does infrastructure play in the great quest for growth and development, and what do the people who plan and build communities want from infrastructure?

Each year, ULI and EY collaborate on an infrastructure report. Our annual reports seek to lay out the infrastructure state of play, to distill broad trends, and to share the best advice from leaders and experts from around the world.

This year, for *Infrastructure 2014: Shaping the Competitive City*, we decided to conduct a survey of global real estate and civic leaders. Our survey sought to answer the following questions:

- How do real estate developers and investors—who could pursue opportunities across cities regionally, nationally, or internationally—think about infrastructure?
- How do city leaders use infrastructure investments to position their cities for real estate investment and economic development?
- What role does infrastructure play relative to other economic development strategies?
- Are public and private perceptions and priorities aligned, or do they diverge, and in what ways?

The answers to these questions might surprise you. What struck us in the findings? Infrastructure is a primary driver of real estate investment. Transit, roads and bridges, and pedestrian infrastructure were important priorities. And cooperation between developers and public leaders is seen as key to delivering infrastructure in the years to come.

We augmented survey findings with interviews and other data points. For more insights into what our research reveals about infrastructure, we invite you to read on.

Patrick L. Phillips
Chief Executive Officer
Urban Land Institute

Howard Roth
Global Real Estate Leader
EY

Contents

Hong Kong's investment in high-quality transit has allowed the city to achieve remarkable densities, a superior quality of life, and protection of environmentally sensitive land areas.

HOW DO REAL ESTATE DEVELOPERS AND INVESTORS—who could pursue opportunities regionally, nationally, or internationally—think about infrastructure? How do city leaders use infrastructure investments to position their cities for real estate investment and economic development? What role does infrastructure play relative to other economic development strategies? And are public and private perceptions and priorities aligned—or do they diverge, and in what ways?

These were the central questions for *Infrastructure 2014: Shaping the Competitive City*, the eighth in an annual series of reports examining infrastructure trends and issues by ULI and EY.

To provide answers, researchers for *Infrastructure 2014* crafted a series of survey questions and asked high-level public officials and private real estate leaders to weigh in. Nearly 250 public sector leaders in local and regional government and over 200 senior-level private developers, investors, and real estate advisers responded to the survey. About 86 percent of survey respondents were based in the United States, with the balance located in countries across the globe.

Nearly every city aspires to grow, and high-quality infrastructure—infrastructure that is well maintained, reliable, safe, resilient, and customer friendly—contributes to well-functioning, growth-primed cities—cities that attract new residents and retain existing ones.

Infrastructure—the physical facilities and systems that support economic activity—is often seen as a driver of real estate and development, especially by those who are in the business of providing it. But do the people actually building and investing in real estate agree? The *Infrastructure 2014* survey tells us "yes"—and a number of other interesting things as well.

On many of the questions asked, there was strong convergence between the public and private sector respondents, and between U.S. and global ones. The survey provides a means for mutual learning and dialogue that can help advance the conversation about the role that infrastructure plays in shaping and promoting growth, infrastructure priorities, and opportunities to improve current practice.

Top Drivers of Real Estate: Infrastructure, Consumer Demand

Infrastructure quality emerged in our survey as the top factor driving where real estate development happens, leading the list of eight possible forces shaping real estate investment.

Eighty-eight percent of survey respondents rated infrastructure quality as a top or very important consideration when determining where real estate investments are made. Infrastructure came out highest for public leaders (91 percent) and second to the top for private leaders (86 percent).

Consumer demand was the top driver for the private sector, with 90 percent of private leaders ranking it a top consideration or very important. A skilled workforce was more likely to be seen as important by the public sector (89 percent) than the private sector (64 percent).

Government services—regulations, tax structure, and quality—fell in the middle of the group of influencing factors for both public and private respondents. However, the private sector saw tax structure as less important than public leaders did, and government quality as more important.

The survey affirms the importance of infrastructure in metropolitan economic development strategies.

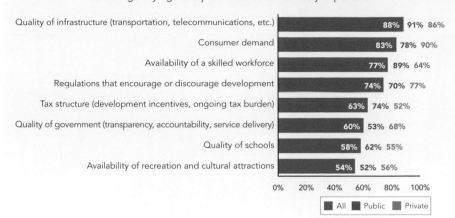

Drivers of Real Estate Investments
Percentage saying "A top consideration" or "Very important"

	All	Public	Private
Quality of infrastructure (transportation, telecommunications, etc.)	88%	91%	86%
Consumer demand	83%	78%	90%
Availability of a skilled workforce	77%	89%	64%
Regulations that encourage or discourage development	74%	70%	77%
Tax structure (development incentives, ongoing tax burden)	63%	74%	52%
Quality of government (transparency, accountability, service delivery)	60%	53%	68%
Quality of schools	58%	62%	55%
Availability of recreation and cultural attractions	54%	52%	56%

Public: In your experience, how important are the following factors in influencing where companies make real estate investments? Private: In your experience, how important are the following factors in influencing where your company makes real estate investments? [Options: A top consideration, Very important, Somewhat important, Not very important, Not a factor at all, Don't know]

Source: *Infrastructure 2014: Shaping the Competitive City* survey.

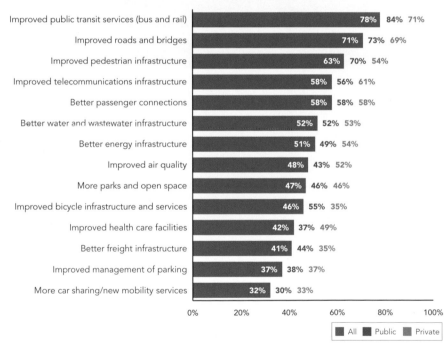

Infrastructure Improvement Priorities
Percentage saying "One of the very top priorities" or "High priority"

	All	Public	Private
Improved public transit services (bus and rail)	78%	84%	71%
Improved roads and bridges	71%	73%	69%
Improved pedestrian infrastructure	63%	70%	54%
Improved telecommunications infrastructure	58%	56%	61%
Better passenger connections	58%	58%	58%
Better water and wastewater infrastructure	52%	52%	53%
Better energy infrastructure	51%	49%	54%
Improved air quality	48%	43%	52%
More parks and open space	47%	46%	46%
Improved bicycle infrastructure and services	46%	55%	35%
Improved health care facilities	42%	37%	49%
Better freight infrastructure	41%	44%	35%
Improved management of parking	37%	38%	37%
More car sharing/new mobility services	32%	30%	33%

Public: Thinking again about the city/metropolitan area where you work, how high a priority do you think should be given to each of these infrastructure improvements over the next ten years? (Please answer for your city/county if you work on that level or the metropolitan area if you work regionally.) Private: Thinking again about the city or metropolitan area where your work is most concentrated, how high a priority do you think should be given to each of these infrastructure improvements over the next ten years? [Options: One of the very top priorities, High priority, Middle priority, Low priority, Bottom priority, Don't know]

Source: *Infrastructure 2014: Shaping the Competitive City* survey.

Highest Infrastructure Priority: Improved Public Transit

Upgrades to public transit systems—including bus and fixed-rail systems—emerged from the survey as a strong priority for future investment. (Transit improvements were unspecified, but could include investments in facilities and capacity, service frequency and reliability, information sharing, and the like.)

Seventy-eight percent of survey respondents saw improved transit services as a top or high priority. Public and private sector respondents were both likely to rank transit as their highest pri-ority, although public leaders were more likely than private ones to rank transit highly (84 percent versus 71 percent).

Transportation-related infrastructure held the top three priority spots, with 71 percent ranking investments

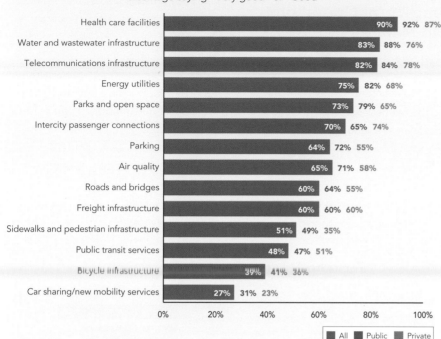

Perceptions of Infrastructure Quality
Percentage saying "Very good" or "Good"

	All	Public	Private
Health care facilities	90%	92%	87%
Water and wastewater infrastructure	83%	88%	76%
Telecommunications infrastructure	82%	84%	78%
Energy utilities	75%	82%	68%
Parks and open space	73%	79%	65%
Intercity passenger connections	70%	65%	74%
Parking	64%	72%	55%
Air quality	65%	71%	58%
Roads and bridges	60%	64%	55%
Freight infrastructure	60%	60%	60%
Sidewalks and pedestrian infrastructure	51%	49%	35%
Public transit services	48%	47%	51%
Bicycle infrastructure	39%	41%	36%
Car sharing/new mobility services	27%	31%	23%

■ All ■ Public ■ Private

Public: Thinking about the city or metropolitan area where you work, how would you rate the current quality of the following aspects of its infrastructure? (Please answer for your city/county if you work at that level -- and for the metropolitan area if you work regionally.) Private: Thinking specifically about the city or metropolitan area where your own work is most concentrated (the place you identified above), how would you rate the current quality of the following aspects of its infrastructure? [Options: Very good, Good, Moderate, Poor, Very poor, Don't know]

Source: *Infrastructure 2014: Shaping the Competitive City* survey.

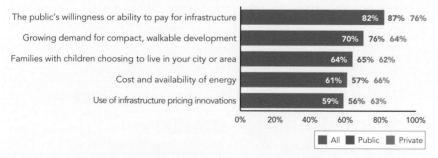

High-Impact Trends and Issues
Percentage saying "Dramatic impact" or "Significant impact"

	All	Public	Private
The public's willingness or ability to pay for infrastructure	82%	87%	76%
Growing demand for compact, walkable development	70%	76%	64%
Families with children choosing to live in your city or area	64%	65%	62%
Cost and availability of energy	61%	57%	66%
Use of infrastructure pricing innovations	59%	56%	63%

■ All ■ Public ■ Private

Public: And over the next ten years, how much of an impact do you think each of the following factors will have in shaping infrastructure and real estate investments in the city or metropolitan area where you work? Private: And over the next ten years, how much of an impact do you think each of the following factors will have in shaping infrastructure and real estate investments in the city or metropolitan area where your work is most concentrated? [Options: Dramatic impact, Significant impact, Some impact, Little impact, No impact, Don't know]

Source: *Infrastructure 2014: Shaping the Competitive City* survey.

Cleveland, Ohio, enhanced mobility with bus rapid transit along the Euclid Avenue corridor. Improvements to the pedestrian realm were an essential component of the project, which has leveraged billions of dollars in real estate investments.

marks in our survey. Roads and bridges received middling marks.

Although many transit systems globally are no doubt of very high quality, increasing ridership coupled with underinvestment has added up to poor conditions in some places.

FINDING 3

Top Trend Shaping Cities: Public Willingness to Pay for Infrastructure

The public's willingness and ability to pay for infrastructure were seen by survey respondents as the most important factor shaping the future of infrastructure and real estate over the next decade. A combined total of 82 percent of respondents—87 percent of public sector and 76 percent of private sector—said that the public's willingness or ability to pay for infrastructure will have a dramatic or significant impact.

This finding points to the need for infrastructure proponents to make a strong, forward-looking case for infrastructure.

Shifting market demands and demographic trends, including growing

in road and bridge infrastructure as a high priority, and 63 percent looking for improved pedestrian infrastructure. Public sector respondents, however, were more likely than private sector ones to see pedestrian and bicycle infrastructure as priorities.

Improving telecommunications was

the third-most-important priority for private sector respondents.

QUALITY Priorities for investment were, in general, the inverse of perceptions of quality. Public transit, pedestrian infrastructure, bicycle infrastructure, and car sharing received the lowest quality

demand for compact, walkable development, and the appeal of cities and metro areas to families with children, were seen as the next two most powerful factors overall. Private sector respondents, however, were likely to think that the cost and availability of energy were more important than demographic shifts.

FINDING 4

Top Infrastructure Funding Source: Cooperation between Developers and Government

Cooperation between developers and local government was identified by three-quarters of respondents as the most significant funding approach for new infrastructure over the next decade. Strategies that require collaboration between real estate and civic leaders—including value-capture and negotiated exactions—also topped the list of likely infrastructure funding sources.

Public and private responses to this question tended to align, despite the limited ability of these strategies to pay for infrastructure at a systematic level and the challenges of applying them in weak-market contexts. Responses to this question reflect the fact that contributions from real estate are often essential components of the funding package for infrastructure projects.

More traditional options, such as income and property taxes and contributions from federal and state governments, were rated as less significant, although every option presented got relatively strong responses, indicating that when it comes to funding, many options need to be on the table.

FINDING 5

Key Concern: Long-Term Operations and Maintenance

When infrastructure investments are planned, how often are long-term operations and maintenance taken into account, and the needed resources identified? Are cities seen as adequately accounting for long-term infrastructure needs?

Our survey shows that both public and private leaders are concerned about how long-term operations and maintenance of infrastructure are resourced.

Overall, 30 percent of survey respondents said that long-term operations and maintenance are usually neglected, with 72 percent saying that operations and maintenance costs were considered some of the time or not at all. Only 25 percent of survey respondents said that long-term operations and maintenance were usually an integrated part of decision making.

Private respondents had a much more pessimistic take on this subject than public sector ones, and global respondents had a more positive view than U.S.-based ones.

Funding Sources for New Infrastructure
Percentage saying "Extremely significant" or "Very significant"

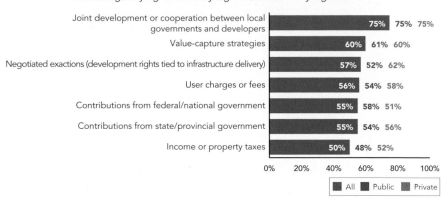

Public: How significant a role do you think each of the following will play in funding new infrastructure investments over the next ten years in the city or metropolitan area where you work? Private: How significant a role do you think each of the following will play in funding new infrastructure investments over the next ten years in the city or metropolitan area where your work is concentrated? [Options: Extremely significant, Very significant, Somewhat significant, Not very significant, Not significant at all, Don't know]

Source: *Infrastructure 2014: Shaping the Competitive City* survey.

Long-Term Operations and Maintenance (O&M)

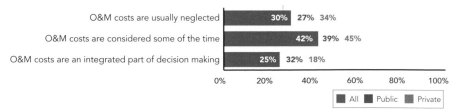

Public: In the city or metropolitan area where you work, do you think enough attention is being paid to allocating resources for long-term operations and maintenance of infrastructure? Private: In the city or metropolitan area where your work is concentrated, do you think enough attention is being paid to allocating resources for long-term operations and maintenance of infrastructure?

Source: *Infrastructure 2014: Shaping the Competitive City* survey. (Percentages do not total 100 due to rounding.)

Shaping the Competitive City

WHEN IT COMES TO REAL ESTATE INVESTMENT, what role does infrastructure play in determining where development happens? How important is it, in relation to other factors like consumer demand, workforce quality, tax policies, and the regulatory environment? And how do civic and real estate leaders think about the quality of various types of infrastructure, and investment priorities for the future?

For *Infrastructure 2014*, we set out to answer these questions and others, in order to build a more complete understanding of how infrastructure fits into the larger real estate investment picture, and to get a sense of what public and private leaders want and expect from infrastructure in the cities they work in and care about.

Nearly every city aspires to grow. High-quality infrastructure—infrastructure that is well maintained, reliable, safe, resilient, and customer friendly—contributes to well-functioning, growth-primed cities, cities that attract new residents and retain existing ones.

Infrastructure—the physical facilities and systems that support economic activity—is often seen as a driver of real estate and development, especially by those who are in the business of providing it. But do the people actually building and investing in real estate agree? This survey tells us "yes"— and a number of other interesting things as well.

On many of the questions asked, there was strong convergence between the public and private sector respondents, and between U.S. and global ones. Where differences emerge, it is hoped that mutual learning and dialogue can help advance the conversation about the role that infrastructure plays in shaping and promoting growth.

METHODOLOGY

Infrastructure 2014: Shaping the Competitive City surveyed key decision makers in the public and private sectors who influence real estate investment in cities and towns in the United States and around the world. Survey respondents included:

- 241 public sector leaders in local and regional government, and private organizations working on local and regional economic development. Public sector officials included elected, appointed, and staff/career representatives.
- 202 private developers, investors, lenders, and advisers, including senior-level executives and managers. Private sector respondents were asked to identify a metropolitan region with which they were familiar, and the location of the region they listed classified them for this survey as U.S. or global.
- Approximately 86 percent of the survey respondents were considered to be U.S.-based respondents; 14 percent were global.

Survey findings were augmented by interviews with survey respondents. Quotes in this report are from those interviews; to encourage candor, quotes have not been attributed.

LEARN MORE

There is much more to learn about what *Infrastructure 2014* tells us about what leaders think about infrastructure. For additional findings, visit www.uli.org/infrastructurereport or www.ey.com/realestate. This site also has more details on survey methodology.

Top Drivers of Real Estate: Infrastructure, Consumer Demand

Many factors stand out as important drivers of real estate investment. These are often thought of as "soft" issues, such as the quality of local schools or other service-oriented facilities, the existence of a skilled workforce, or the availability of regulatory incentives such as tax breaks.

But in the ULI/EY survey of global real estate and public leaders, infrastructure quality emerged as the top factor in driving where real estate development happens, leading the list of eight possible forces shaping real estate investment for the survey respondents overall.

Eighty-eight percent of survey respondents ranked infrastructure quality as a top or very important consideration when determining where real estate investments are made, with infrastructure coming out highest for public leaders (91 percent) and second to the top for private leaders (86 percent).

Consumer demand was primary for the private sector, with 90 percent of private leaders ranking it a top consideration or very important. A skilled workforce was more likely to be seen as important by the public sector (89 percent) than the private sector (64 percent).

Government services—regulations, tax structure, and quality—fell in the middle of the group of influencing factors for both public and private respondents. However, the private sector saw tax structure as less important than private leaders saw it, and government quality as more important.

Global and U.S. respondents tended to agree in their responses, although global respondents were more likely to cite government-related factors— including the regulatory environment and the quality of government—as considerations, and were less likely to be concerned about schools.

HIGH-IMPACT INFRASTRUCTURE CATEGORIES

What infrastructure categories tend to matter the most, when it comes to where real estate investments happen? Survey respondents were likely to put strong telecommunications systems and connectivity; sufficient, well-maintained roads and bridges; reliable and affordable energy; and good intercity passenger connections at the top of the list.

Telecommunications includes high-speed internet and other services. Today's real estate

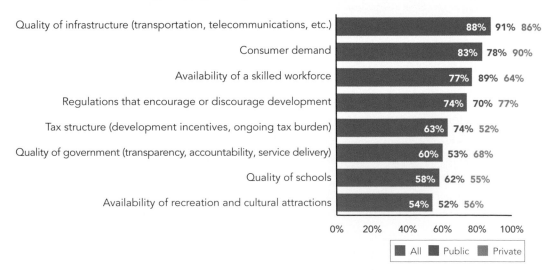

Drivers of Real Estate Investments
Percentage saying "A top consideration" or "Very important"

	All	Public	Private
Quality of infrastructure (transportation, telecommunications, etc.)	88%	91%	86%
Consumer demand	83%	78%	90%
Availability of a skilled workforce	77%	89%	64%
Regulations that encourage or discourage development	74%	70%	77%
Tax structure (development incentives, ongoing tax burden)	63%	74%	52%
Quality of government (transparency, accountability, service delivery)	60%	53%	68%
Quality of schools	58%	62%	55%
Availability of recreation and cultural attractions	54%	52%	56%

Public: In your experience, how important are the following factors in influencing where companies make real estate investments? Private: In your experience, how important are the following factors in influencing where your company makes real estate investments? [Options: A top consideration, Very important, Somewhat important, Not very important, Not a factor at all, Don't know]

Source: *Infrastructure 2014: Shaping the Competitive City* survey.

consumers expect reliable and high-quality access to wireless networks. "Bandwidth," one hospitality executive noted, "is absolutely essential."

Although public transit is in the middle of the list of the infrastructure factors that influence where real estate investments happen, transit was a key investment priority for survey respondents, as seen below.

Some interviewees noted that while infrastructure is essential, high-quality systems are also largely assumed to be in place, especially in urban areas. Water, electricity, telecommunications, and other services are part of the package of infrastructure elements that well-functioning cities provide. Differentiators then become proximity to transport, especially high-quality transit, good roads and bridges, and, for some real estate sectors, airport and passenger connections.

THE INFRASTRUCTURE EQUATION

What explains the emphasis on infrastructure? On the public side, there is a strong understanding of the extent to which the provision of infrastructure can be used to support greater densities. One public leader in the United States said, "Anytime we engage in redevelopment strategies, we are aware of the role that infrastructure can [play] and will use it to facilitate or encourage private sector investment."

On the private side, the calculation is aimed more at the bottom line. Developers have seen how good infrastructure can support property values. What's more, developers today are more likely to have to pay the costs of infrastructure improvements associated with their proposed projects.

According to one developer, "When we're redeveloping or rezoning, if infrastructure is substandard then it becomes part of the development process or the rezoning process, and we end up having to bear some of the cost." In that case, developers may rethink the project. The cost of infrastructure improvements must get priced into the deal, and market conditions will determine whether a project proceeds.

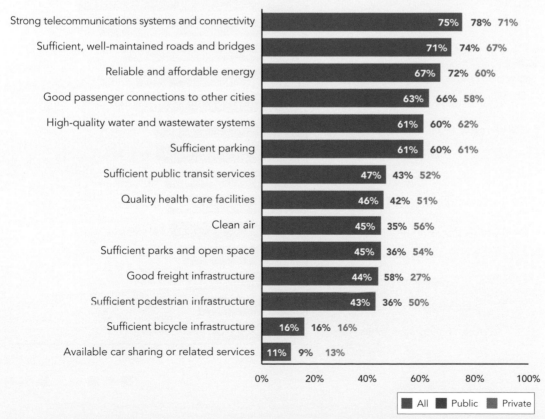

Infrastructure-Related Factors in Real Estate
Percentage saying "A top consideration" or "Very important"

Factor	All	Public	Private
Strong telecommunications systems and connectivity	75%	78%	71%
Sufficient, well-maintained roads and bridges	71%	74%	67%
Reliable and affordable energy	67%	72%	60%
Good passenger connections to other cities	63%	66%	58%
High-quality water and wastewater systems	61%	60%	62%
Sufficient parking	61%	60%	61%
Sufficient public transit services	47%	43%	52%
Quality health care facilities	46%	42%	51%
Clean air	45%	35%	56%
Sufficient parks and open space	45%	36%	54%
Good freight infrastructure	44%	58%	27%
Sufficient pedestrian infrastructure	43%	36%	50%
Sufficient bicycle infrastructure	16%	16%	16%
Available car sharing or related services	11%	9%	13%

■ All ■ Public ■ Private

Public: And in your experience, how important are the following infrastructure-related factors in influencing where companies make real estate investments? Private: And in your experience, how important are the following infrastructure-related factors in influencing where your company makes real estate investments? [Options: A top consideration, Very important, Somewhat important, Not very important, Not a factor at all, Don't know]

Source: *Infrastructure 2014: Shaping the Competitive City* survey.

Highest Infrastructure Priority: Improved Public Transit

One of the most striking themes to emerge from both the survey and the interviews was a focus on upgrading public transit systems—including bus and fixed-rail systems—as a strong priority for future investment. (Transit improvements were unspecified, but could include investments in facilities and capacity, service frequency and reliability, information sharing, and the like.)

Seventy-eight percent of survey respondents saw improved transit services as a top or high priority. Public and private sector respondents were both likely to rate transit as a high priority, although public leaders were more likely than private ones to rank transit highly (84 percent versus 71 percent). In the open-ended questions at the end of our survey, the need to invest more in transit was frequently mentioned.

Global respondents were more likely to prioritize transit services than U.S. respondents, with 84 percent saying that sufficient public transit was a top consideration or very important.

Transportation-related infrastructure held the top three priority spots, with 71 percent rating investments in road and bridge infrastructure as a high priority, and 63 percent looking for improved pedestrian infrastructure. (Public sector respondents, however, were more likely than private sector ones to see pedestrian and bicycle infrastructure as priorities.)

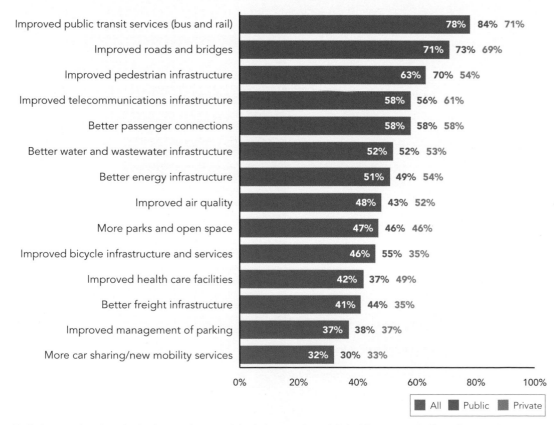

Infrastructure Improvement Priorities
Percentage saying "One of the very top priorities" or "High priority"

	All	Public	Private
Improved public transit services (bus and rail)	78%	84%	71%
Improved roads and bridges	71%	73%	69%
Improved pedestrian infrastructure	63%	70%	54%
Improved telecommunications infrastructure	58%	56%	61%
Better passenger connections	58%	58%	58%
Better water and wastewater infrastructure	52%	52%	53%
Better energy infrastructure	51%	49%	54%
Improved air quality	48%	43%	52%
More parks and open space	47%	46%	46%
Improved bicycle infrastructure and services	46%	55%	35%
Improved health care facilities	42%	37%	49%
Better freight infrastructure	41%	44%	35%
Improved management of parking	37%	38%	37%
More car sharing/new mobility services	32%	30%	33%

■ All ■ Public ■ Private

Public: Thinking again about the city/metropolitan area where you work, how high a priority do you think should be given to each of these infrastructure improvements over the next ten years? (Please answer for your city/county if you work on that level or the metropolitan area if you work regionally.) Private: Thinking again about the city or metropolitan area where your work is most concentrated, how high a priority do you think should be given to each of these infrastructure improvements over the next ten years? [Options: One of the very top priorities, High priority, Middle priority, Low priority, Bottom priority, Don't know]

Source: *Infrastructure 2014: Shaping the Competitive City* survey.

Infrastructure Quality Perceptions and Investment Priorities

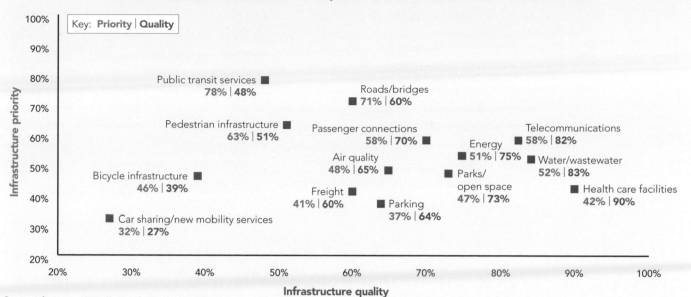

Key: **Priority | Quality**

Public transit services
78% | 48%

Roads/bridges
71% | 60%

Pedestrian infrastructure
63% | 51%

Passenger connections
58% | 70%

Telecommunications
58% | 82%

Energy
51% | 75%

Air quality
48% | 65%

Water/wastewater
52% | 83%

Bicycle infrastructure
46% | 39%

Parks/
open space
47% | 73%

Health care facilities
42% | 90%

Freight
41% | 60%

Parking
37% | 64%

Car sharing/new mobility services
32% | 27%

Infrastructure priority (y-axis)

Infrastructure quality (x-axis)

Source: *Infrastructure 2014: Shaping the Competitive City* survey.

Perceptions of Infrastructure Quality

Percentage saying "Very good" or "Good"

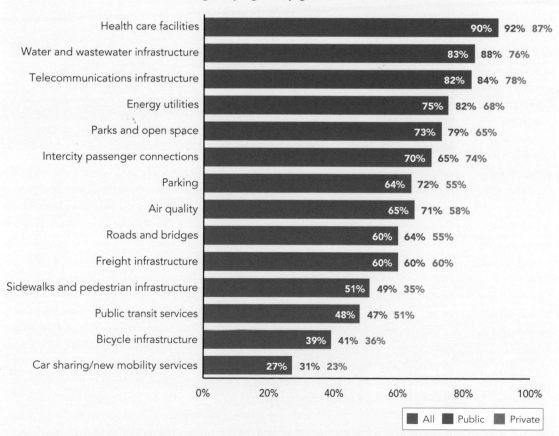

	All	Public	Private
Health care facilities	90%	92%	87%
Water and wastewater infrastructure	83%	88%	76%
Telecommunications infrastructure	82%	84%	78%
Energy utilities	75%	82%	68%
Parks and open space	73%	79%	65%
Intercity passenger connections	70%	65%	74%
Parking	64%	72%	55%
Air quality	65%	71%	58%
Roads and bridges	60%	64%	55%
Freight infrastructure	60%	60%	60%
Sidewalks and pedestrian infrastructure	51%	49%	35%
Public transit services	48%	47%	51%
Bicycle infrastructure	39%	41%	36%
Car sharing/new mobility services	27%	31%	23%

■ All ■ Public ■ Private

Public: Thinking about the city or metropolitan area where you work, how would you rate the current quality of the following aspects of its infrastructure? (Please answer for your city/county if you work at that level — and for the metropolitan area if you work regionally.) Private: Thinking specifically about the city or metropolitan area where your own work is most concentrated (the place you identified above), how would you rate the current quality of the following aspects of its infrastructure? [Options: Very good, Good, Moderate, Poor, Very poor, Don't know]

Source: *Infrastructure 2014: Shaping the Competitive City* survey.

Improving telecommunications was the third-most-important priority for private sector respondents, perhaps reflecting telecommunications' significance as a driver of real estate activity.

INFRASTRUCTURE QUALITY

Priorities for investment are, in general, the inverse of perceptions of quality. Pedestrian infrastructure, public transit, bicycle infrastructure, and car sharing received the lowest quality marks in our survey, with roads and bridges receiving middling marks.

When it comes to assessing infrastructure quality, public and private sector respondents were in general agreement about which are the best and the worst. This was true from top to bottom, although the public sector participants tended to give higher marks to most of the elements.

The link between transit and pedestrian infrastructure—and current perceptions of poor quality for both—help explain the desire to invest in and upgrade these infrastructure services. Other factors driving these priorities could be growing densities in urban areas, environmental sensitivities, and the cost of driving and parking.

CASE STUDY

Investing in Port Connections: Port of Miami's Tunnel Project

MIAMI IS INCREASING ACCESS to its port and benefiting its downtown by using a public/private partnership (PPP) to construct a tunnel directly linking the highway and the port with the Interstate Highway System.

The Port of Miami Tunnel Project, a $1 billion project that began construction in May 2010 and is scheduled to open in May 2014, will provide new access to the Port of Miami by creating a direct line between Interstate 395 and the port. Two tunnels that provide eastbound and westbound access will relieve congestion in the region and benefit the downtown by allowing truck and freight traffic to bypass congested surface streets.

Prior to the project, the Port of Miami, which is located on Dodge Island in Biscayne Bay and owned by Miami–Dade County, was connected to the mainland only by the Port Bridge, which can be accessed on the mainland only by downtown surface streets. Upon completion, approximately 4,400 trucks per day will be able to bypass local surface streets and access the port directly from Interstate 395.

The Port of Miami is Miami–Dade County's second-largest economic generator, and the tunnel project is expected to help improve the competitiveness of the port in the wake of improvements to the Panama Canal. According to port director Bill Johnson, the Port of Miami has a goal of doubling its cargo traffic over the next

several years, which will add jobs at the port and in related logistics, industrial, and professional industries. The expansion of the port, which includes improved access due to the tunnel project, dredging the bay to accommodate the larger post-Panamax ships, and the installation of new "super cranes," has an estimated economic impact of $27 billion.

The tunnel project is also expected to reduce congestion on downtown surface streets, improving safety on these streets for other users and increasing economic activity in the city's central business district.

The $1 billion cost for the tunnel project is being financed through a PPP among the Florida Department of Transportation (FDOT), Miami–Dade County, the city of Miami, and Miami Access Tunnel (MAT)

Concessionaire LLC, which is owned by a Meridian investment fund and Bouygues Travaux Publics, the lead contractor for the project. The 35-year agreement includes the design, construction, financing, operations, and maintenance of the tunnel. MAT will be responsible for the operation and maintenance of the tunnel upon completion, and will receive availability payments for this service, subject to meeting performance criteria contained in the concession agreement. The tunnel will be returned to FDOT at the end of the concession agreement.

No tolls will be charged for the use of the tunnel, so as not to divert traffic back to the existing bridge or affect the economics of the port. Instead, Miami–Dade County is providing a portion of the project's funding.

Transportation Habits of Americans

Percentage doing at least weekly

	Gen Y	Gen X	Baby boomers	Older generations
Driving	90%	95%	94%	85%
Taking public transit	20%	7%	10%	4%
Walking to a destination	47%	46%	43%	31%
Biking	19%	16%	12%	6%

Source: *ULI America in 2013* survey.

Although many transit systems globally are no doubt of very high quality (see the Hong Kong case study), increasing ridership coupled with underinvestment has added up to poor conditions in some places. Many cities are making aggressive investments in transit, and the results of the survey support these efforts.

TRANSIT AND THE PUSH TOWARD DENSITY

Demographic shifts are at play here, and are driving a need to dramatically upgrade and expand infrastructure categories that may not have been priorities in the past. According to a developer in the southern United States: "Young professionals are moving back [to the city] in record numbers; [they] are more transit-oriented. But it's not just rail; they like to walk and bike as well. So the vast majority of development that has occurred over the last decade in this city has been in either transit-friendly or walkable environments."

In developed countries, market demand for higher-density living in city cores works in tandem with local government desires to become more financially efficient by concentrating urban development in areas with high-quality transit. As a result, according to one city planner, "We are intensifying density across the metro area, which is focusing the development [of] and investment in infrastructure." Across the United States, many cities are investing in major transit upgrades.

Improved public transit is also important in developing markets such as those in Asia, although for different reasons. There, ongoing urbanization is drawing ever more people from rural areas into cities already overcrowded and choked with traffic. With these problems only set to worsen, economies structurally underserved in transit infrastructure must now make major investments to avoid gridlock.

Given the high cost of installing new rail networks, planners are also looking to make more cost-effective transit improvements, often aimed at improving efficiency. Better interconnections between different transport networks were mentioned repeatedly in interviews. Smart solutions using new technology also featured prominently.

CAR SHARING

When it came to quality, car sharing received low marks in our survey, perhaps reflecting the limited reach of those services at this time. Interviewees suggested they lacked "critical mass" in many places. With more progressive cities in pursuit of a variety of "new mobility" approaches, however, current policy initiatives may accelerate their uptake.

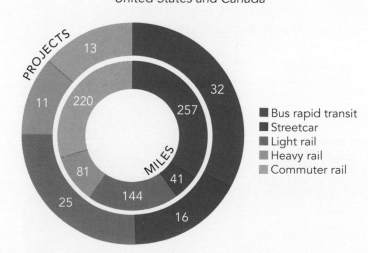

Transit Projects under Construction in 2014
United States and Canada

PROJECTS: 13, 11, 220, 81, 25, 32

MILES: 257, 41, 144, 16

- ■ Bus rapid transit
- ■ Streetcar
- ■ Light rail
- ■ Heavy rail
- ■ Commuter rail

Source: The Transport Politic.

Interview | Gabe Klein

GABE KLEIN IS THE FORMER TRANSPORTATION CHIEF for the cities of Chicago and Washington, D.C. He is known for spearheading efforts to make cities less car-centric and more people-friendly. Klein served as a regional vice president for Boston-based car-sharing company Zipcar from 2002 through 2006. He is a senior visiting fellow for ULI in 2014.

You're known as an innovator in urban transportation. What have been the greatest advancements in the last ten years?

The last ten years have seen a resurgence of cities across the board. When I moved to Washington, D.C., in 1995, it was still in a state of decline. In that case, a combination of stabilizing finances and a more professional management team set the stage for the innovations that you have seen over the last decade, and I think that goes for many U.S. cities. So with that as a basis, drops in crime rates, combined with a strategy for reinvestment in cities, have created an environment for economic growth, the potential for population growth, and it all feeds on itself.

I was in the private sector ten years ago with Zipcar, and then, like now, both public and private have been driving each other to innovate. When car sharing started to really take off in Washington, Boston, New York City, and then West Coast cities, I think that was a turning point. You had young people wanting to move to cities and starting to do the economic analysis on the back of an envelope and saying, "It is going to cost more to rent in the city, but the transportation options are such that I don't 'have to' spend $1,000 a month on my personal transportation."

The heavy-rail and bus systems represent the backbone of the public transportation system but not the entirety of it. I think government realized that [it] could support "soft transportation" options that were perhaps provided by the private sector versus public, by providing free or subsidized on-street parking, marketing, and utilizing services themselves.

This then led to more sharing innovations like bike sharing that could be led by the government, in partnership with the private sector. There has been a big movement toward active transportation as well. Biking, for instance, is the most popular recreational sport in the United States. But it has been a leap to see the bicycle as transportation again.

The investment by cities in cycling infrastructure, wider sidewalks, and streetscapes has reinvigorated urban economies by creating a sense of place, and essentially putting back in place what made cities attractive to residents in the first place, and why cities in Europe never lost their dominance. We also saw U.S. cities looking to Europe for what was working, like streetcars, light rail, and bus rapid transit, for instance.

In a nutshell, we have been rebuilding the social fabric in cities by rebuilding the basics of the transportation systems undone by urban renewal and other factors, and in tandem creating places again with streetscapes and other physical enhancements that are basically what the public is asking for.

Can you look into your crystal ball and tell us what's around the bend?

In many ways, the planning crisis of the 1950s [through the] 1980s was just that, temporary, and now we are getting back on track. Each success in

Worldwide Car Sharing

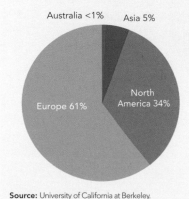

2006
346,610 worldwide members
11,696 worldwide vehicles
Percentage of worldwide membership

Australia <1% Asia 5%
Europe 61% North America 34%

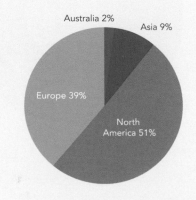

2012
1,788,027 worldwide members
43,554 worldwide vehicles
Percentage of worldwide membership

Australia 2% Asia 9%
Europe 39% North America 51%

Source: University of California at Berkeley.

Washington, Chicago, New York, or Memphis is painting a picture for politicians, activists, businesses, and residents that you can believe in, change you can see with your own two eyes. This is why implementation is so important. Enough talk, let's walk.

Over the next ten years, we are going to build on our strengths even more, get more density, and provide more layers of services for residents and businesses. In Washington, for instance, we have seen consistent growth in population and decline in auto registrations. This is due to public and private innovations.

Over the next ten years, I think the private sector will be relied on much more to provide services as exponential innovation is happening and government needs the private sector to keep up with the change. Autonomous cars, private buses, and other innovations will change the landscape so quickly that taxis, ride share, [and] car sharing as we know them will cease to exist. Government needs to play an active role in policy to make sure that these changes are positive for cities, and that the greater good is always prioritized.

Many cities struggle to build the hard infrastructure to support biking, walking, car-sharing, and other mobility choices. Is technology the easy part? In a perfect world, how do technology and physical infrastructure interact?
This is an article unto itself! They are both über-important. I am fascinated by the nexus of physical and virtual. An app by itself is interesting, but usually only insomuch as it can interact with our daily lives, whether it be delivering a good or service, a car to our door, a bikeshare bike, or a train ticket. The hard infrastructure is, well, hard to build. It's not easy to alter a street and add a bike lane, or change the sidewalk width. It takes political will, money, planning and design, and more.

What's the future of parking?
I am so proud of what we accomplished in D.C. with parking policy, including technology, with the highest penetration of payment by phone in the world. Having said that, I am very excited about parking basically "going away" by the end of this decade.

Cars currently sit 95 percent of the time on average. Car-sharing vehicles sit less, but still a majority of the time in a day. With autonomous cars, the prediction is that cars will move 95 percent of the time and be disengaged 5 percent of the time (only to get maintenance and gas).

No one will own a car in a city, which has huge ramifications for the car industry and all related industries as I laid out above, but also for parking itself! All that storage will no longer be needed. This is hugely exciting for cities and urban planners, as all of that storage space can be used for people again! This also has ramifications for city revenues from parking, taxi medallions, and lots of other things but is a net-net positive. Did I mention we won't lose 32,000 people a year to traffic accidents?

What did your time as head of transportation for D.C. and Chicago teach you? If you had one bit of advice for city transportation directors, what would it be?
Stop saying "no" and start saying "maybe, why, and let's figure out how." Playing it safe is no recipe for success. Don't be afraid to experiment, represent it that way, and make the public part of your experiment in some cases. With the environmental crises we are facing, the competition among cities, and the demand for services, there is no more time to waste.

People in government often bend when it gets hard. They prioritize the bureaucracy over the innovation and public need. Not everyone, of course—I have worked with some amazing people. But there are not a lot of leaders out there who say, "Let's do this because it is the right thing to do," and then are able to put together the coalition of support, budget, and plans to get the done. At the end of the day, getting it done is what matters.

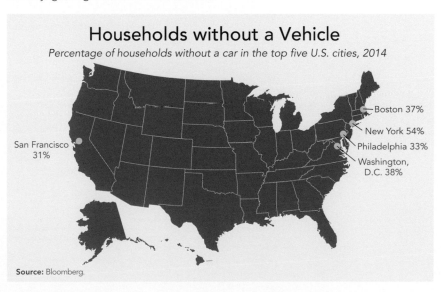

Households without a Vehicle
Percentage of households without a car in the top five U.S. cities, 2014

San Francisco 31%

Boston 37%
New York 54%
Philadelphia 33%
Washington, D.C. 38%

Source: Bloomberg.

Top Trend Shaping Cities:
Public Willingness to Pay for Infrastructure

The public's willingness to pay for infrastructure is seen by survey respondents as the most important factor shaping the future of infrastructure and real estate over the next decade. Whether funding for infrastructure is collected via taxes (income, sales, property, etc.), user fees like tolls, or other means, how the public feels about these levies greatly affects how much money is collected.

The public's willingness or ability to pay for infrastructure is viewed as more important than most other cultural and technological factors churning now. A combined total of 82 percent of respondents (87 percent of public sector and 76 percent of private sector) said this factor will have a dramatic or significant impact on infrastructure investments.

Shifting market demands and demographic trends, including growing demand for compact, walkable development, and the appeal of cities and metro areas to families with children, are seen as the next two most powerful factors overall. Private sector respondents, however, were likely to think that the cost and availability of energy were more important than demographic shifts.

Though no doubt significant in some places, climate change and extreme weather events were seen by just 37 percent of survey respondents as important infrastructure-shaping forces. Global respondents were more likely than U.S. respondents to see climate change as significant—60 percent of them said climate change and extreme weather events would have a dramatic or significant impact.

Willingness and ability to pay are influenced by a variety of factors, including economic conditions and perceptions of debt and government. That public willingness and ability to pay came out so strongly points to the need for infrastructure proponents to:

■ Make a strong, forward-looking case about the need for investment;

■ Develop messages that resonate with the public, and find other ways to generate public support for infrastructure;

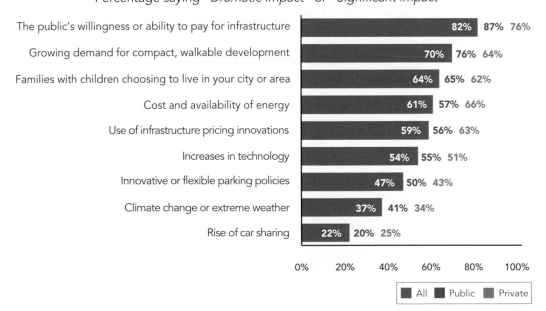

Trends and Issues Shaping Cities
Percentage saying "Dramatic impact" or "Significant impact"

	All	Public	Private
The public's willingness or ability to pay for infrastructure	82%	87%	76%
Growing demand for compact, walkable development	70%	76%	64%
Families with children choosing to live in your city or area	64%	65%	62%
Cost and availability of energy	61%	57%	66%
Use of infrastructure pricing innovations	59%	56%	63%
Increases in technology	54%	55%	51%
Innovative or flexible parking policies	47%	50%	43%
Climate change or extreme weather	37%	41%	34%
Rise of car sharing	22%	20%	25%

Public: And over the next ten years, how much of an impact do you think each of the following factors will have in shaping infrastructure and real estate investments in the city or metropolitan area where you work? Private: And over the next ten years, how much of an impact do you think each of the following factors will have in shaping infrastructure and real estate investments in the city or metropolitan area where your work is most concentrated? [Options: Dramatic impact, Significant impact, Some impact, Little impact, No impact, Don't know]

Source: *Infrastructure 2014: Shaping the Competitive City* survey.

- Identify cost-effective infrastructure investment strategies; and
- Carefully steward resources when projects are approved.

In the face of challenging economic times, with many economies around the world still digging out from recession, it is difficult to ask people to pay more for anything. And in the United States in particular, a gloomy economic atmosphere has combined with an increasingly politically charged conversation about government and taxes. As one city leader said, "Washington has become ideologically driven—you can't even discuss increasing taxes. And if you can't have the discussion, how can you reach a rational conclusion?" As a public good, infrastructure is implicated when sentiment turns against government.

Other factors exacerbate the problem. Recent lower economic growth means that national and local economies are unable to generate the same levels of tax revenue as they once did. And local public pension obligations are squeezing spending on other needs in some places.

But there are exceptions to every rule. Some communities have managed to persuade the public that paying for infrastructure is a worthwhile endeavor, and lessons from those places are worth paying attention to.

Ballot measures to fund infrastructure continue to perform well at the polls in the United States, especially when the efforts paint a bold, positive vision for the future. Ballot efforts that succeed motivate voters by coupling stories about deep infrastructure needs with an inspirational vision about what investments in infrastructure can help communities achieve.

Infrastructure may be a key driver of real estate investment, but answering the question of how communities will foot the bill for it remains a work in progress.

U.S. Transportation Ballot Measures

2013 results	2012 results
8 states	17 states
15 measures	62 measures
Approved: 11	Approved: 49
Rejected: 4	Rejected: 13
Success rate: 73%	Success rate: 79%

Source: Center for Transportation Excellence.

Top Infrastructure Funding Source: Cooperation between Developers and Government

In many places—and notably the United States—traditional revenue strategies, such as the gas tax for transportation, have been stagnant or in decline. What alternative approaches are seen as promising by survey respondents?

Three-quarters of both public sector and private sector leaders identified cooperation between developers and local government, or joint development, as the most significant funding approach for new infrastructure over the next decade.

Strategies that require collaboration between real estate and civic leaders top the list of likely infrastructure funding sources. Six in ten respondents expected value-capture strategies to play a significant role. Over half thought that negotiated exactions—in which development rights are tied to the delivery of infrastructure projects—will also be an important funding source.

More traditional options—such as income and property taxes, and contributions from federal and state governments—were rated as less significant, although every option presented got relatively strong responses, indicating that when it comes to funding, many options will need to be on the table.

Public and private responses to this question tended to align, despite the limited ability of development-driven strategies to pay for infrastructure at a systematic level and the challenges of applying them in weak-market contexts. These answers demonstrate that private sector investors and developers recognize that they will need to do their part to catalyze new infrastructure investment. Revenues from real estate—though a small part of the overall infrastructure funding picture—can be essential components of the funding package for specific projects, like transit lines or stations.

If the trend is toward expecting developers to provide more infrastructure, not all interviewees were in support. Some developers complained that local governments are now asking them to pay an unreasonable share of infrastructure costs. Another developer commented: "There is clearly a public commitment necessary to encourage the type of development pattern that will be best for a particular city or municipality. The private sector can't fund it all, especially after this recession. And if you think about it, isn't it better to have mixed-use, higher-density development even if the development can't pay for any public improvements?"

Funding Sources for New Infrastructure
Percentage saying "Extremely significant" or "Very significant"

	All	Public	Private
Joint development or cooperation between local governments and developers	75%	75%	75%
Value-capture strategies	60%	61%	60%
Negotiated exactions (development rights tied to infrastructure delivery)	57%	52%	62%
User charges or fees	56%	54%	58%
Contributions from federal/national government	55%	58%	51%
Contributions from state/provincial government	55%	54%	56%
Income or property taxes	50%	48%	52%

Public: How significant a role do you think each of the following will play in funding new infrastructure investments over the next ten years in the city or metropolitan area where you work? Private: How significant a role do you think each of the following will play in funding new infrastructure investments over the next ten years in the city or metropolitan area where your work is concentrated? [Options: Extremely significant, Very significant, Somewhat significant, Not very significant, Not significant at all, Don't know]

Source: *Infrastructure 2014: Shaping the Competitive City* survey.

Other interviewees noted the limits of expecting strategies like value capture, including tax increment financing and special assessments, to pay for infrastructure at a systematic level. These strategies are typically focused on particular projects or in particular areas, and generate traction because "people are prepared to pay if they can see what they are paying for." Mastering the cooperation frameworks needed to make joint development and other coordinated approaches work will be essential.

In general, interviewees also voiced a preference for adopting more of a "user-pay" approach, possibly via public/private partnerships. However, local governments, facing pressure from constituents to keep infrastructure fees low, may be more inclined to migrate toward use of more conventional means of raising revenue, such as municipal bonds backed by general revenues. "The problem with that from a municipal perspective is that it further divorces the value created by infrastructure from the things that ought to be paying for the maintenance of it," said one interviewee.

CASE STUDY

Linking Transit and Land Use: The Hong Kong Model

By intentionally linking real estate and transit, and developing land around its stations, the Hong Kong transit system has been able to achieve exceptional transit service, compact land use patterns around the city, and profitability.

The Hong Kong transit system boasts some impressive statistics, including a 99.9 percent on-time percentage, low-cost fares (an average of $1 per ride), and a farebox recovery rate for operations of 185 percent—the world's highest. The system carries 5.1 million passengers daily and has trains arriving every two minutes or less during peak hours. It's also highly profitable, producing revenues in 2012 of 36 billion Hong Kong dollars (about US$5 billion), and a profit of 2 billion HKD. How has the system been able to achieve all of this?

Hong Kong's Mass Transit Railway Corporation, or MTR, is not just a transit provider. The corporation is also a developer. MTR is able to take advantage of the value created by transit investments by developing land above and around its stations, generating revenues that have allowed MTR to fund transit expansions and upgrades and ensure that the system runs smoothly and efficiently, further boosting ridership.

Over the last decade, over half of MTR's operating revenue has come from property development rather than transportation service provision. The model that MTR uses is a rail-property (R+P) model. MTR purchases development rights from the government—its primary shareholder—at "before rail" prices. It then uses the value captured through developing that land or selling or leasing the land to another developer to pay for transit investments. Many stations in the city are tied to Hong Kong shopping centers and mixed-use developments owned by MTR.

This model rests on the understanding that a transit system is more than just a means of transportation. At its best, transit provides the land use structure for an efficient city, and underpins its overall well-being. By linking high-quality transit and land development, Hong Kong has been able to achieve remarkable densities, a superior quality of life, and protection of environmentally sensitive land areas.

The MRT enjoys leeway in land acquisition and real estate development that few other transit agencies do. But joint development and value capture are strategies that cities and transit agencies in many places are adopting. According to Jay Walder, the chief executive officer of MTR, connections between transit and land use should be kept in mind when considering what 21st-century cities can be.

Key Concern:
Long-Term Operations and Maintenance

When infrastructure investments are planned, how often are the costs of long-term maintenance and operations taken into account, and the needed resources identified? Are cities seen as adequately accounting for long-term infrastructure needs? Our survey confirms that both public and private leaders are concerned about how long-term operations and maintenance of infrastructure are resourced.

Overall, 30 percent of survey respondents said that long-term operations and maintenance are usually neglected, with 72 percent saying that operations and maintenance costs were considered some of the time or not at all. Only 25 percent of survey respondents said that long-term operations

and maintenance were usually an integrated part of decision making.

This was one of the few questions in the survey where public and private perceptions diverged significantly. Just 32 percent of public sector survey respondents said that forward planning for infrastructure maintenance and operations is incorporated as an integrated part of decision making, but the message from the private sector was even starker, with 18 percent saying that adequate provision is currently being made in their cities.

Global respondents tended to be more sanguine than U.S.-based ones, with 34 percent of global leaders saying that long-term consider-

Long-Term Operations and Maintenance (O&M)

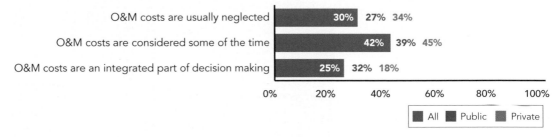

Public: In the city or metropolitan area where you work, do you think enough attention is being paid to allocating resources for long-term operations and maintenance of infrastructure? Private: In the city or metropolitan area where your work is concentrated, do you think enough attention is being paid to allocating resources for long-term operations and maintenance of infrastructure?

Source: *Infrastructure 2014: Shaping the Competitive City* survey. (Percentages do not total 100 due to rounding.)

Long-Term Operations and Maintenance (O&M)

U.S. vs. Global Presence

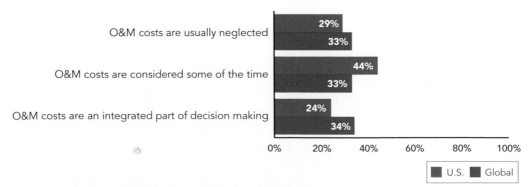

Public: In the city or metropolitan area where you work, do you think enough attention is being paid to allocating resources for long-term operations and maintenance of infrastructure? Private: In the city or metropolitan area where your work is concentrated, do you think enough attention is being paid to allocating resources for long-term operations and maintenance of infrastructure?

Source: *Infrastructure 2014: Shaping the Competitive City* survey. (Percentages do not total 100 due to rounding.)

Building Infrastructure to Last: the London Olympics

IN LONDON, the 2012 Olympic Games provided the opportunity for the city to upgrade infrastructure and revitalize disinvested neighborhoods. Careful planning and investments laid the groundwork for sustained impact.

The legacy of the Olympic Games is one of celebrated stadiums, spaces, and structures becoming neglected and dilapidated once the games are over. The organizers of the 2012 London summer Olympics, however, determined that London would be the exception to the rule—they have made it a priority to plan for and create infrastructure and buildings with lasting value.

Site selection was the first key consideration. Organizers chose a 617-acre (250 ha) brownfield site as home for the London Olympic Park, in order to take advantage of a prime opportunity to clean up the postindustrial debris in the site area and spur development in the adjacent, economically struggling boroughs of East London. Extensive planning laid the groundwork for a long-term strategy focused on the infrastructure and development legacy of the games.

The London transit network was substantially upgraded in preparation for the games, with Transport for London investing £6.5 billion in ten railway lines and 30 bridges. Connections to East London—an area that has suffered from underinvestment in both housing and infrastructure—were improved throughout the system. This investment was used to upgrade and expand the existing system, increasing capacity and improving service.

The region's urban and suburban train network, the London Overground, extended service on the East London and North London lines and upgraded signaling, trains, and stations. A new cable car, the Emirates Air Line, provides a Thames River crossing in East London and can carry 2,500 people per hour (though post-Olympics usage has been lower than anticipated).

In addition to transit system upgrades, a £10 million investment was used to build or improve 47 miles (75 km) of pedestrian and cycling infrastructure on eight key

routes that connect London communities to the site and link with networks that serve other parts of the city. Improvements included widening bike lanes, improving road crossings, adding a wayfinding system, and creating new bike parking spaces in central London. In addition, the London bike-share system added 2,300 bikes before the games, increasing the number of bikes in the system by nearly 50 percent.

The Olympic Park site, which is set to fully reopen in the spring of 2014 as Queen Elizabeth Olympic Park, will provide a venue for sports and entertainment as well as one of Europe's largest urban parks, complete with lawns, gardens, trees, meadows, and wetlands.

Two bridges in the park—an important component of the new pedestrian and cy-

cling infrastructure—will span the wetlands and link east and west. These bridges have permanent and temporary sections: the temporary sections handled high-volume crowds during the games, and have been removed in order for new plantings to flourish, while the permanent sections remain to meet legacy requirements.

The London games adopted a theme of long-term sustainability. As a result, the infrastructure built for the games was designed to benefit the neighborhood after the games were over. The results have been positive: areas close to the site have seen construction in new multifamily housing progress faster over the past few years than almost anywhere else in the United Kingdom.

ations are usually integrated, compared with 25 percent of all respondents. This may refect the greater global prevalence of long-term public/ private partnerships and the use of whole life cycle costing in many global markets.

When infrastructure is not operated and maintained properly, efficiency deteriorates, safety can be challenged, and other problems result. High-quality standards during construction can mitigate long-term resource needs, but only to a point.

According to one U.S.-based interviewee, "The crucial issue going forward is not so much the ability to install infrastructure, but how to maintain it. The sprawling development pattern that historically took place here requires a lot of infrastructure maintenance for what is a low level of development."

A city leader in the American Sunbelt expanded on that theme. "Two-thirds of our streets have been built by developers in the past 30 years. They are now owned by the city. They're relatively new, but costs will rise over time. There will come a time when we're going to be facing the same situa-

tion that older cities face. We need to be putting money aside, and have a plan for dealing with it."

Although changes to public funding strategies aimed at resolving the maintenance issue have been slow to emerge, the prospect of an impending problem is serving as a further catalyst for the trend toward more densely populated metropolitan areas.

According to one interviewee: "The old model of low-density development doesn't offer the efficiencies or the returns to support ongoing operations and maintenance of infrastructure investment, and one way [to address] this is via the increasing densification of our city."

Another, more controversial approach is simply to cut loose areas that can't be cost-effectively maintained. But this has obvious drawbacks.

Clearly, something has to change, although one private sector interviewee talked about the bright side of our collective short-sightedness. "If people really thought through the long-term implications," he joked, "nothing would ever get built."

Conclusion

CITIES EVERYWHERE ARE BALANCING MULTIPLE PRIORITIES, and must make hard choices about the allocation of scarce resources. *Infrastructure 2014: Shaping the Competitive City* affirms the primacy of high-quality infrastructure as a key attractor of real estate investment dollars and activity. As cities and metropolitan areas think about how to position themselves for growth and development, smart infrastructure choices have to be part of the mix.

What do these choices look like? Leaders in our survey name public transit and pedestrian infrastructure like good sidewalks as top contenders for infrastructure dollars. Both lag in the quality rankings, and are sought-after commodities by key demographic segments, like generation Y. Upgrading the quality of roads and bridges—long-neglected assets in many places—would help complete the transportation package, especially if they were built to accommodate many different kinds of users.

Funding for infrastructure, our survey respondents say, rests largely on how willing the public is to pay for it. Communities must overcome reluctance to fund infrastructure at adequate levels, and make sure that they are building a strong case for infrastructure of the right kind, in the right places. Cooperation between the development community and the public sector, our survey suggests, will be an essential part of the mix going forward.

Every infrastructure and real estate investment is a long-term one. Too often, however, how to pay for upfront capital costs dominates the conversation about infrastructure projects. Private sector leaders in particular worry about the long-term operations and maintenance of infrastructure assets.

Infrastructure 2014 confirms that stakeholders need to better understand the return on investment that infrastructure and land use decisions have, and the impact of those decisions on public coffers over the long term. To prosper in the future, jurisdictions need to successfully communicate the benefits and returns of infrastructure investments to the public, master the cooperation needed for joint development, and account for the revenue to appropriately maintain and operate infrastructure.

Recognizing the connections between infrastructure and real estate can lead not only to new funding and partnership models, but also to better planning of cities and prioritization of projects. Through dialogue between the public and private sectors about perspectives and priorities, the role that infrastructure plays in shaping and promoting growth can be better understood and capitalized upon.

We invite you to learn more at www.uli.org/infrastructurereport and www.ey.com/realestate.

Notes

CURRENCY

All currency is given in U.S. dollars, unless otherwise noted.

SURVEY

Two hundred forty-one public sector leaders in local and regional government and private organizations working on economic development, along with 202 private developers, investors, lenders, and advisers took part in the infrastructure survey in January 2014.

A survey invitation was sent by e-mail to leaders identified by ULI and EY. The list of survey recipients was constructed using contacts and connections developed by ULI and EY, and augmented by a search of publicly available information for senior public officials in major cities around the world.

The public sector invitees are high-level leaders—elected, appointed, and career—from large and mid-sized cities in the United States, Europe, the Asia Pacific region, and elsewhere. The public representatives who received the survey have responsibilities for overall city affairs, transportation, public works, planning, economic development, and other city functions. Also included in the public sector list were leaders from regional bodies, such as metropolitan planning organizations, chambers of commerce, and other entities set up to promote city and metropolitan development.

The private sector mailing list included senior-level executives and managers in real estate development, investment, advisory, or related real estate firms in the United States and overseas. The real estate industry recipients are based in countries around the world, with concentrations in the United States, Europe, and the Asia Pacific region.

Infrastructure investors and other private sector people typically involved in infrastructure delivery (such as engineering or construction firm executives) were excluded. Public leaders working at the state and national levels were excluded.

An e-mailed letter from ULI CEO Patrick Phillips and EY Global Real Estate Leader Howard Roth invited the leaders to take part in the survey, and asked them to click on a link to the questionnaire. Several reminders were sent to nonresponders, and questionnaires were returned between January 7 and 24, 2014. The findings were analyzed by Belden Russonello Strategists and responses treated confidentially. Some respondents volunteered to be recontacted for a follow-up interview.

QUOTES

ULI and EY conducted 35 interviews for this report. All interviewees completed the survey. All unattributed quotes are from these conversations.

Interviewees

Scott Adams
Deputy City Manager
City of Las Vegas, Nevada

David Allman
Founder and Chairman
Regent Partners

Richard Bickle
Director of Planning
Delaware Valley Regional Planning
   Commission

Timothy Bowen
Executive Director–Middle East
Costain Limited

Ken Bowers
Deputy Planning Director
City of Raleigh, North Carolina

Aaron Cain
Planning Supervisor
City of Durham, North Carolina

Brian Collins
Head of Development
Fisher Brothers

Rick Dishnica
President
The Dishnica Company LLC

John Dudas
Vice President
Belz Enterprise

Jim Durrett
Executive Director and Board Member
Buckhead Community Improvement
   District
Metropolitan Atlanta Rapid Transit
   Authority

Thomas Gibson
Senior Vice President and Partner
Holladay Properties

Dean Grandin
Director of City Planning
City of Orlando, Florida

Gerard Groener
CEO
Corio N.V.

David Henry
Chief Executive Officer
Springfield Land Corporation

Nirmal Kotecha
Director of Capital Programme and
   Procurement
U.K. Power Networks

Stephen Lawler
Director, Group Retail Development
Value Retail PLC and S.D. Malkin
   Properties

Austin Ley
Manager, Strategic Research
City of Melbourne, Australia

David Livesley
Chief of Staff and Transformation
   Director (Former)
Cross Rail Ltd.

Brian Ludicke
Planning Director
City of Lancaster, California

John Mant
City Councillor
City of Sydney, Australia

Lauralee Martin
President and CEO
HCP Inc.

Gary Molyneaux
Manager, Airport Planning and Program
   Development
King County International Airport

Kjersti Monson
Director, Long-Range Planning
City of Minneapolis, Minnesota

Peter Pappas
President and Managing Partner
Pappas Properties LLC

Philip Payne
Principal and Chief Executive Officer
Gingko Residential

Danny Pleasant
Director of Transportation
City of Charlotte, North Carolina

Victoria Quinn
City Councillor
City of Birmingham, United Kingdom

Jim Robertson
Manager, Urban Design Division
City of Austin, Texas

Struan Robertson
Executive Vice President and Chief
   Investment Officer
Host Hotel & Resorts

Scott Shapiro
Managing Director
Eagle Rock Ventures

Mike Slevin
Director, Environmental Services
   Department
City of Tacoma, Washington

Kathy Sokugawa
Chief Planner
City and County of Honolulu, Hawaii

Bill Trumbull
General Manager, Real Estate
Chicago Transit Authority

Almis Udrys
Deputy Chief of Staff
City of San Diego, California

Smedes York
Chairman
York Properties Inc.

Sponsoring Organizations

THE URBAN LAND INSTITUTE is a nonprofit research and education organization whose mission is to provide leadership in the responsible use of land and in creating and sustaining thriving communities worldwide.

The Institute maintains a membership representing a broad spectrum of interests and sponsors a wide variety of educational programs and forums to encourage an open exchange of ideas and sharing of experience. ULI initiates research that anticipates emerging land use trends and issues and provides advisory services; and publishes a wide variety of materials to disseminate information on land use development.

Established in 1936, the Institute today has over 32,000 members and associates from some 92 countries, representing the entire spectrum of the land use and development disciplines. Professionals represented include developers, builders, property owners, investors, architects, public officials, planners, real estate brokers, appraisers, attorneys, engineers, financiers, academics, students, and librarians.

ULI relies heavily on the experience of its members. It is through member involvement and information resources that ULI has been able to set standards of excellence in development practice. The Institute is recognized internationally as one of America's most respected and widely quoted sources of objective information on urban planning, growth, and development.

ULI SENIOR EXECUTIVES

Patrick L. Phillips
Chief Executive Officer

Cheryl Cummins
Executive Officer

Michael Terseck
Chief Financial Officer/Chief
   Administrative Officer

Jason Ray
Chief Technology Officer

Lela Agnew
Executive Vice President,
   Communications

Kathleen B. Carey
Executive Vice President/Chief Content
   Officer

David Howard
Executive Vice President, Development
   and ULI Foundation

Joe Montgomery
Chief Executive, Europe

Marilee Utter
Executive Vice President, District Councils

John Fitzgerald
Senior Vice President and Executive
   Director, Asia Pacific

URBAN LAND INSTITUTE
1025 Thomas Jefferson Street, NW
Suite 500 West
Washington, DC 20007-5201

Phone: 202-624-7000
www.uli.org